Christmas
Treasury

*Stories, poems and carols
selected by Victoria Parker*

**BARDFIELD
PRESS**

First published by Bardfield Press in 2004
Bardfield Press is an imprint of
Miles Kelly Publishing Ltd
Bardfield Centre, Great Bardfield, Essex, CM7 4SL

2 4 6 8 10 9 7 5 3 1

Editorial Director: Belinda Gallagher

Editor: Kate Miles

Designer: Louisa Leitao

Picture Researcher: Liberty Newton

Production Manager: Estela Boulton

British Library Cataloguing-in-Publication Data
A catalogue record for this book is available from the British Library

ISBN 1-84236-385-9

The publishers would like to thank the following artists whose
work appears in this book:
Martin Angel, Julie Banyard, Vanessa Card, Louisa Leitao,
Diana Mayo, Tracy Morgan, Peter Utton, Mike White
Cover: Peter Dennis/Linda Rogers Associates

The illustration on page 62 © The British Library/HIP/TopFoto.co.uk
Other images from Corel, Digital Stock, ILN, Dover Publications, PhotoDisc

Printed in China

www.mileskelly.net
info@mileskelly.net

Contents

Stories

Poems & Rhymes

Songs & Carols

Stories

. . . And Joseph also went up from Galilee, from the city of Nazareth to Judea, to the city of David, which is called Bethlehem, because he was of the house and lineage of David, to be enrolled with Mary, his betrothed, who was with child. And while they were there, the time came for her to be delivered. And she gave birth to her first-born son and wrapped him in swaddling cloths, and laid him in a manger, because there was no place for them in the inn . . .

(Luke 2: 2-7)

Christmas is based on one of the most famous stories in the world – the tale of the nativity from the Bible. Many captivating myths and legends have since grown up around the festival, explaining traditions such as the origin of Santa Claus, the reason for Christmas trees, and how the first tinsel was magicked from spiders' webs. Besides a wealth of wonderful folktales, the Christmas season has provided classic stories from some of the best-loved writers in the world, such as Hans Christian Andersen and Charles Dickens. The following selection of tales from around the world has been specially compiled to inspire and entertain.

Babushka

A Russian folktale

There was great excitement in the village where Babushka lived. All the old lady's neighbours were out of doors, peering up at the wintry night sky, where the biggest star anyone had ever seen was shining down at them. "Where has it come from?" everyone gasped in astonishment. "What does it mean?"

Babushka stayed indoors, getting on with her housework as usual. "What a lot of fuss about a star!" she muttered to herself as she swept and dusted, scrubbed and mopped, polished and tidied. "I haven't got time to waste, I've got standards to keep up." Babushka's house was always spotless and in perfect order.

RAT-TAT-TAT! came a loud knocking at the door.

"Now who's that interrupting my work?" Babushka frowned.

She hurried to the door, plumping up the cushions and tidying a vase of flowers on the way. Three foreign-looking men were standing on the doormat, wrapped in long robes and swathed in turbans. Even more surprisingly, the camels they had been riding were tied to the gatepost and were snorting steam into the cold air.

Babushka

"Good evening, Babushka," the first man greeted her. He held out his hand and it jingled with bangles of gold, while jewelled rings sparkled on his fingers.

"We are travelling from a far distant country, and we need a place to rest for the night. Would you be kind enough to welcome us in?" Babushka could see that the men were rich and important.

"Of course . . . I would be honoured," she spluttered red-faced, and she welcomed her guests into her little sitting room while she quickly untied her apron and smoothed down her hair. "What brings you to these parts?" Babushka asked politely, as she bustled about lighting a fire.

"We are following the strange star that shines so brilliantly," the second man explained.

"Really?" smiled Babushka, as she went to bring three plates of bread and cheese and pickles from the kitchen.

Babushka

"We believe that it will lead us to a new king – the king of all Heaven and Earth," continued the third man.

"Well, fancy that!" remarked Babushka, scurrying to fetch three steaming mugs of hot chocolate.

"Why don't you come with us, Babushka?" the first man urged. "We leave tomorrow with gifts of gold, frankincense and myrrh."

"Thank you, but I can't possibly come with you," said Babushka. "If I were to go away, who would air the beds and sweep the stairs and dust the shelves and scour the sink? Besides, I don't have anything that would be suitable as a gift for a king!"

"This king is newborn," the second man said kindly. "He is still only a tiny baby."

Babushka paused with a tray full of washing-up. "I had a baby boy once," she said in a whisper, "but he died."

The third man rose to his feet and put his hand gently on Babushka's arm. "Come with us," he said, softly. "Come with us to see the baby saviour of the world."

Babushka stood and thought. Her eyes had a faraway look in them and there was a sad smile on her lips. "Maybe just this once . . ." she murmured to herself. Suddenly – CUCKOO! CUCKOO! CUCKOO! – the clock in the hall noisily broke the silence.

"Oh dear, is that the time?" cried Babushka, springing back into action. "I must make up the guest beds!" and she rushed up the stairs.

Babushka

Next evening, the star was brighter and higher in the sky.

"Are you sure you won't come with us, Babushka?" the three men asked as they mounted their camels ready to go.

"I've got too much to do," the old lady blustered.

The three men waved sadly as they lurched away. Babushka's heart was strangely heavy as she shut the door and went back inside her little cottage. She left her broom standing in the corner, the washing-up in the sink and the crumbs under the table, and she went and unlocked a cupboard in the corner of the sitting-room instead. Babushka sighed a deep sigh as she gazed at the shelves in front of her. They were stacked with toys of every size and colour. Babushka ran her fingers lovingly over them, wiping off a layer of dust.

"My little son's toys would make a perfect present for the new king," she said.

It took Babushka all night to wash, dry and polish the toys, until each one was as good as new. As the sun came creeping through her window, she packed the toys in a bag, put on her coat and headscarf, opened her door and locked it behind her. Then she was off down the path.

Babushka walked and walked and walked – through villages, towns and cities. She lost track of time, but she noticed one night that the star faded from the sky.

Babushka

A few days later, she came to the little town of Bethlehem.

"Have you seen three men on camels, looking for a baby?" Babushka asked a local innkeeper.

"Why, yes," replied the innkeeper. "The three men were here all right. In fact, the baby was born in that very stable over there." He pointed to a dingy hut at the back of his inn. "The three men didn't stay long – just as well, really, because just after they'd gone, a group of shepherds came to see the baby too."

The innkeeper laughed.

"It would have been a bit crowded with everyone there at once! But I'm afraid you're a bit too late. After all the visitors had gone, the parents left with their baby last week." Babushka looked from the empty stable to her full bag of toys.

"I will go on searching until I find the baby," she decided. "I will give him my presents and ask him if he will be my king too." Then she turned on her heel and strode away determinedly . . .

Babushka is still wandering over the world today, looking for the baby king. No one notices her as she goes quietly from house to house, but whenever she sees a good girl or boy, she dips into her shopping bag and places a toy by their bed. It is only on one day every year that the children find Babushka's gifts – and that is Christmas Day, the birthday of Jesus, the baby in the stable.

The Nutcracker Prince

Retold from the original tale by Ernst Hoffman

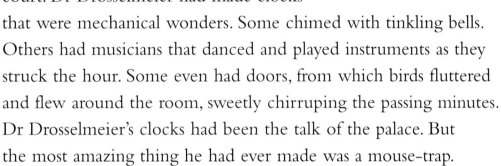

Dr Drosselmeier was an old man with a secret. In his youth, he had been the most nimble-fingered, highly skilled craftsman in the royal court. Dr Drosselmeier had made clocks that were mechanical wonders. Some chimed with tinkling bells. Others had musicians that danced and played instruments as they struck the hour. Some even had doors, from which birds fluttered and flew around the room, sweetly chirruping the passing minutes. Dr Drosselmeier's clocks had been the talk of the palace. But the most amazing thing he had ever made was a mouse-trap.

Dr Drosselmeier had invented a clockwork trap that caught mice in their hundreds, twenty-four hours a day. Everyone had been delighted – except for the Mouse King. He too had lived in the palace with his subjects. Now he was forced to find another home. The Mouse King knew powerful magic and he took his revenge on Dr Drosselmeier by turning his nephew into an ugly, wooden doll. The doll wore a painted soldier's uniform and it had a prince's crown painted onto its head. Its jaws moved so it could crack nuts between its teeth. The Mouse King's spell was so strong that there was only one way to undo it.

Firstly, the nutcracker prince had somehow to kill the Mouse King. Secondly, a little girl had to love him, in spite of his ugliness. Well, Dr Drosselmeier had no idea where the Mouse King had gone, and he didn't know a little girl kind enough to take pity on the ugly, wooden doll. So his nephew stayed a nutcracker.

From that moment on, Dr Drosselmeier had never made another clock. He lost heart for mechanical things and so he lost his job at the palace. Dr Drosselmeier blamed himself for his nephew's disappearance and he had never breathed a word of what had happened to anyone. But ever since, he had been trying to find a way to break the Mouse King's spell, and at last, he thought he had.

Dr Drosselmeier's goddaughter, Clara, had grown into the kindest little girl anyone could wish to meet. If anyone was going to take pity on the stiff, glaring nutcracker prince, it would be Clara.

It was Christmas Eve. Dr Drosselmeier had arrived at Clara's house trembling with excitement. He wasn't excited because there was a party going on. No, Dr Drosselmeier was excited because tonight was the night he hoped the magic would be undone and his nephew would return to life. While the party guests talked and joked and laughed together, Dr Drosselmeier set about emptying the huge bag he had brought with him. It was filled with gingerbread and shortcake, candy walking sticks and sugar

pigs, nuts and bon bons, nougat and humbugs . . . High and
low, in every corner of the room, Dr Drosselmeier heaped
piles of the Mouse King's favourite foods. That should tempt
him out from wherever he's hiding, thought Dr Drosselmeier.

Then it was time to give Clara her Christmas present. The
little girl's eyes opened wide with excitement as she stripped
off the sparkly paper. But her face suddenly fell as she saw the
ugly nutcracker prince. Then, gently, Clara stroked the doll's
face. He wasn't cute, he wasn't cuddly – he wasn't even new!
But that was exactly why Clara loved him. She couldn't bear
to think of leaving him alone, laughed at and unloved –
especially at Christmas. Clara clutched the nutcracker
prince and hugged him. And Dr Drosselmeier slipped
away from the party, his heart light with hope . . .

When the party was over and it was bedtime at last, Clara
tucked the wooden doll up next to her. "I love you," she whispered,
just before she fell asleep. And that night, Clara had a strange dream.
She dreamt that the nutcracker prince woke up beside her. He
smiled at Clara and held her hand, and led her downstairs. There
was scuffling and squeaking coming from the drawing room, and
when Clara peeped around the door she saw there were mice
everywhere! They were climbing all over Dr Drosselmeier's goodies,
fighting and biting each other to get at the sweets. Worst of all,
a seven-headed mouse was cackling with glee at all the arguing
and the mess. The seven-headed mouse wore seven
golden crowns and Clara could tell that he must
be the king of the mice.

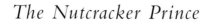

The Nutcracker Prince

The nutcracker prince bravely charged at the Mouse King with a sword in his hand and began to fight furiously. But he was completely outnumbered. The mice swarmed to their king's defence. They dragged the nutcracker prince to the ground and he disappeared under a thousand biting, clawing bodies. Just as the Mouse King began to laugh, Clara tore off her slipper and threw it at him with all her might. WHAM! It hit the Mouse King on four of his seven heads. He staggered to and fro, and then collapsed dead to the floor.

When the mice saw that their leader was dead, they scooped up his body and then they were gone, streaming through cracks in the wall, holes in the skirting and gaps in the floorboards.

The nutcracker prince ran to Clara and kissed her. "Thank you for all you have done for me," he whispered. "Let me repay you by taking you on a journey to my kingdom, the realm of sweets."

It was the most wonderful dream Clara had ever had. She travelled through forests made of barley sugar, crossed rivers that ran with lemonade, picked flowers of sherbert, walked on paths of chocolate, and visited the nutcracker prince's gingerbread castle. In fact, Clara was sorry to be woken up – even though it was Christmas Day! She hugged the wooden doll and told him, "You're the best present I've ever had." She could have sworn that his smile was broader than usual.

Meanwhile, across the city, Dr Drosselmeier had also woken up to find the best present he'd ever had. Beneath his Christmas tree, sleeping peacefully, was his nephew.

Why the Robin has a Red Breast

An Inuit legend

In the land where it is always winter, there
once lived a man and his son. It was so cold that they lived in
a house made of snow, and their clothes were made of fur.

But even with the warm furs it was cold in the snow house.
The man and his son had a fire, too. They needed the fire to heat
the snow house. They needed it to have hot food to eat. So they
never let their fire go out, as without it they would surely die.

Whenever the father went out hunting, he would leave his son
with a great pile of wood. The fire burned brightly by the entrance
to the snow house. The first thing the boy had learned was never
ever to let the fire go out.

Now one of the creatures the man was always hunting was the
great white bear. The great white bear hated the man and used all
his cunning to hide from the hunter.

The bear saw that the fire was precious to the man and his
son. He thought that if only he could stamp out
the fire with his huge white paws, the man
and his son would fall into such a deep
cold sleep that they would never wake
again. So the great white bear watched
and waited for his chance.

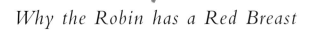

Why the Robin has a Red Breast

One day the father fell ill. All day he tossed and turned on his bed. He was not able to go out hunting. The great white bear watched as the son fed the fire with sticks as his father had taught him. The next day, the father was no better. The son looked after him as well as he could but by now he was growing hungry. At night he could hear the great white bear prowling round the snow house, and he was afraid. The third day the father hardly moved at all, and the boy had to fight to keep his eyes open. He put some more sticks onto the fire, but eventually he could keep his eyes open no longer. He fell into a deep, deep sleep.

The great white bear pounced. He stomped and stamped and put the fire out with his huge white paws. Then he padded away, leaving the boy and his father to their fate. It grew bitterly cold in the snow house. Frost and snow gathered round the furs on the bed, and round the boy's furry hood. Still he slept on and on. Both father and son grew stiff with cold.

The boy had one special friend. It was a tiny little brown bird called a robin. The boy used to feed the robin and let it shelter in the snow house when the blizzards blew. The little bird came hopping up to the snow house and he saw right away that all was not well. He twittered round the boy's head, calling to warn him that the fire had gone out. But still the boy slept on, exhausted by all his efforts to look after his father. The robin scratched among the ashes where the great white bear had stomped, desperately

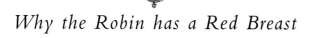
looking for just one tiny ember that was still alight. He found one tiny spark, and he began fanning it with his little wings. He flapped his wings for all he was worth and slowly, slowly the flame caught. It spread to another piece of stick, and still the robin flapped and flapped his wings. The heat was growing now, and the robin's feathers were scorching. More and more sticks caught alight, and the brave little robin felt his chest feathers burn red with heat.

The boy woke with a start and leapt to his feet. He saw the fire was nearly out, and he rushed to pile on more sticks. He did not see his tiny friend flutter off into the darkness outside. It grew warmer in the snow house, and to his great joy the boy saw his father was stirring on the bed. His eyes were clear and the sickness had passed. In the distance, the great white bear stumped off a long way from the snow house. He could see he was not going to get the better of the hunter and his son.

The next time the robin came to the snow house for food, the boy was puzzled to see the little brown bird now had a bright red breast. But he was never to know why.

The Little Match Girl

From the original tale by Hans Christian Andersen

It was New Year's Eve and bitterly cold. Snow and ice lined the streets like an untrodden white carpet, for all the people were indoors, happily preparing to bring in the New Year. All alone in the windy square by the fountain, the poor girl who sold matches shivered. She pulled her ragged shawl a little closer around her thin cotton dress. She rubbed her hands together and blew on her fingers and stamped her feet, but freezing wet snow came swamping through the holes in her boots.

The little matchgirl hadn't sold one box of matches all day and she was too frightened to go home, for her father would be extremely angry. "Someone will surely pass this way and buy in a minute," she told herself. But how cold she was, how cold! "If only I could light one of my matches," she murmured, "that would warm me a little." With fingers stiff with cold, the little matchgirl falteringly took out one of her matches and struck it.

The tiny wooden splinter blazed into a bright little flame and the little matchgirl cupped her hands over it, craving its spark of warmth and light. As she stared into the orange centre of the flame, she saw herself standing in front of a

The Little Match Girl

roaring stove, giving out heat that warmed her from the tips of her toes to the top of her head. Suddenly, the match's flame went out and the vision died with it. The little matchgirl somehow felt even colder than before.

The little matchgirl didn't dare light another match for a long time. Then "Just one more," she whispered, through her chattering teeth. Shaking, the little matchgirl drew out another of her precious wares and struck it on the wall. The glimmer from the little matchstick seemed to light up the stone until it was clear and glassy, like a crystal window. Through the window, the little matchgirl could see a room with a welcoming fire and bright candles and a table laden with delicious things to eat, and she held out her hands towards it. It seemed as if she was going to be able to reach right through the glass and into the wonderful room – then the match died out. The magical room vanished, and huge tears filled the little matchgirl's eyes.

Her poor numb hands fumbled to light another, and her pale face lit up with wonder in the glow of the third flame. Suddenly a magnificent Christmas tree sparkled before the little matchgirl in the light. It shimmered with glassy balls of many colours and glittered with tinsel, and tiny dots of candlelight danced all over its thick green needles. "How beautiful!" said the little matchgirl, her eyes big and round. Then the flame from the match scorched her fingers and she dropped it,

black and twisted, into the snow. The Christmas tree was gone, but the glimmering lights from its candles were still there, rising up and up into the night sky until they mingled with the twinkling stars. Suddenly, one of the lights fell through the darkness, leaving a blazing trail of silver behind it. "That means someone is dying," the little matchgirl murmured, remembering what her Granny used to say whenever they saw shooting stars.

As the little matchgirl stood dreaming of her beloved, dead grandmother, she unthinkingly lit up another match – and there was her granny before her in the light of the flame. "Granny, don't go!" sobbed the little matchgirl, as she lit one match after another, so the vision wouldn't fade like all the others. "Let me stay with you!" she begged, and the old lady smiled and held out her arms for the little matchgirl to run into, just as she always had done.

It was midnight, and all over the city the church bells pealed out to welcome in the New Year. Revellers poured out of the inns and houses to dance and sing and shake hands with strangers and wish each other well. There, lying in the snow by the fountain, was a little girl's thin, lifeless body, surrounded by spent matches. For the little matchgirl had left it there when she had gone away with her grandmother. She had no need of it in the place where they were going: a place without cold, nor hunger, nor pain – just happiness.

The Christmas Tree Fairy of Strasburg

A German folktale told by J Stirling Coyne

O nce, long ago, there lived near the city of Strasburg a
handsome count named Otto. As the years flew by he
remained unwed. For this reason people began to call him
'Stone Heart.'

One Christmas Eve Count Otto ordered that a great hunt take
place. He and his guests rode forth, and the chase became more and
more exciting. It led through thickets and forests until Count Otto
was separated from his companions.

He rode alone until he came to a spring of clear, bubbling
water, known to the local people as the Fairy Well. Here Count
Otto dismounted and began to wash his hands. To his wonder he
found that though the weather was cold the water was warm. As he
plunged his hands deeper, he fancied that his right hand was
grasped by another, soft and small, which slipped from his finger
the gold ring he always wore. When he drew out his hand, the
gold ring was gone.

The count mounted his horse and returned to his castle,
resolving that the next day he would have the Fairy Well emptied.
He retired to his room and tried to sleep but the strangeness of the
day kept him awake. Suddenly he heard the baying of the hounds in
the courtyard and then the slow creaking of the drawbridge,

as though it were being lowered. Then came the patter of small feet on the stone staircase, and next he heard footsteps in the chamber adjoining his own.

Count Otto sprang from his couch, and as he did so there sounded a strain of music, and the door of his chamber was flung open. Hurrying into the next room, he found himself in the midst of fairy beings, clad in sparkling robes. They paid no heed to him, but began to dance, laugh and sing.

In the centre of the room stood a splendid Christmas tree, the first ever seen in that country. Instead of toys and candles there hung on its branches stars, necklaces, bracelets and jewels. The whole tree swayed, sparkled, and glittered.

Count Otto stood speechless when suddenly the fairies stopped dancing and made room for a lady of dazzling beauty who came slowly towards him.

She wore on her head a golden crown set with jewels. Her hair flowed upon a robe of rosy satin and creamy velvet. She stretched two small, white hands to the count and said, "Dear Count Otto, I come to return your Christmas visit. I am Ernestine, the Queen of the Fairies. I bring you something that you lost in the Fairy Well."

And as she spoke she drew from her bosom a golden casket, set with diamonds, and placed it in his hands. He opened it eagerly and found within his lost gold ring.

Overcome by an irresistible impulse, the count pressed the Fairy Ernestine to his heart, while she drew him into the magic mazes of the dance. The music floated through the room, and the rest of the fairies whirled around the Fairy Queen and Count Otto, and then dissolved into a mist of colours.

Then the young man fell to his knees before the Fairy Queen and asked her to be his bride. She consented on the condition that he should never speak the word 'death' in her presence. The next day the wedding of Count Otto and Ernestine, Queen of the Fairies, was celebrated with great pomp. The two continued to live happily together for many years.

One day the count and his wife were going hunting in the forest around the castle. The horses were saddled and bridled and the count paced the hall in great impatience; but still the Fairy Ernestine remained in her chamber. At length she appeared and the count addressed her in anger.

"You have kept us waiting so long," he cried, "that you would make a good messenger to send for death!"

Scarcely had he spoken the forbidden word, when the Fairy, vanished from his sight. In vain Count Otto searched the castle and the Fairy Well, but no trace could he find of his wife but the imprint of her hand set in the stone arch above the castle gate.

Many years passed by, and the Fairy Ernestine did not return. Every Christmas Eve the count placed a lighted tree in the room where he had first met her, hoping that she would return to him.

Time passed and the count died. The castle fell into ruins. But to this day, on the arch above the gate, can be seen the imprint of a hand, and such, say the good folk of Strasburg, was the origin of the Christmas tree fairy.

Poems & Rhymes

Over the centuries Father Christmas has been known by many names, and countless stories have been told about him around the world. Today, children picture Father Christmas as a jolly old man whizzing around the world in a sleigh pulled by reindeer, delivering toys – all thanks to a poem. *The Night Before Christmas* was written by a New York professor of Bible studies, Clement Clarke Moore, for his children in 1822. It was published a year later and gained such widespread and enduring popularity that Moore's image of Father Christmas has become the familiar figure loved by millions today.

Poems and rhymes are traditionally an important part of Christmas. For instance, at the end of the 19th century, to round off Christmas Day in Britain, children would recite a poem to their relatives as entertainment. And many favourite Christmas carols started out as poems, being set to music later. For centuries, poems have been a perfect way of capturing the magic and mystery of the Christmas season.

The Night Before Christmas

Clement Clarke Moore

'Twas the night before Christmas, when all through the house
Not a creature was stirring, not even a mouse;
The stockings were hung by the chimney with care,
In hopes that St Nicholas soon would be there;
The children were nestled all snug in their beds,
While visions of sugar plums danced in their heads;
And mamma in her 'kerchief, and I in my cap,
Had just settled our brains for a long winter's nap,
When out on the lawn there arose such a clatter,
I sprang from the bed to see what was the matter.
Away to the window I flew like a flash,
Tore open the shutters and threw up the sash.

The Night Before Christmas

The moon on the breast of the new-fallen snow
Gave the lustre of midday to objects below,
When, what to my wondering eyes should appear,
But a miniature sleigh, and eight tiny reindeer,
With a little old driver, so lively and quick,
I knew in a moment it must be St Nick.
More rapid than eagles his coursers they came,
And he whistled, and shouted, and called them by name:
'Now, Dasher! now, Dancer! now, Prancer and Vixen!
On, Comet! on, Cupid! on, Donner and Blitzen!
To the top of the porch! To the top of the wall!
Now dash away! Dash away! Dash away all!'
As dry leaves that before the wild hurricane fly,
When they meet with an obstacle, mount to the sky,
So up to the house-top the coursers they flew,
With the sleigh full of toys, and St Nicholas too.

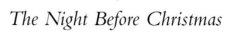

And then, in a twinkling, I hear on the roof
The prancing and pawing of each little hoof.
As I drew in my head, and was turning around,
Down the chimney St Nicholas came with a bound.
He was dressed all in fur, from his head to his foot,
And his clothes were all tarnished with ashes and soot;
A bundle of toys he had flung on his back,
And he looked like a peddler just opening his pack.
His eyes – how they twinkled, his dimples how merry!
His cheeks were like roses, his nose like a cherry!
His droll little mouth was drawn up like a bow,
And the beard of his chin was as white as the snow;
The stump of a pipe he held tight in his teeth,
And the smoke it encircled his head like a wreath;
He had a broad face and a little round belly,
That shook, when he laughed, like a bowlful of jelly.
He was chubby and plump, a right jolly old elf,
And I laughed when I saw him, in spite of myself;

The Night Before Christmas

A wink of his eyes and a twist of his head,
Soon gave me to know I had nothing to dread;
He spoke not a word, but went straight to his work,
And filled all the stockings, then turned with a jerk,
And laying his finger aside of his nose,
And giving a nod, up the chimney he rose;
He sprang to his sleigh, to his team gave a whistle,
And away they all flew like the down of a thistle.
But I heard him exclaim, ere he drove out of sight,
'Happy Christmas to all, and to all a good night.'

In the Bleak Midwinter

Christina Rossetti

In the bleak midwinter, frosty wind made moan,
Earth stood hard as iron, water like a stone;
Snow had fallen, snow on snow, snow on snow,
In the bleak midwinter, long ago.

Our God, heaven cannot hold him, nor earth sustain;
Heaven and earth shall flee away when he comes to reign.
In the bleak midwinter a stable place sufficed
The Lord God Almighty, Jesus Christ.

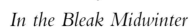

In the Bleak Midwinter

Angels and archangels may have gathered there,
Cherubim and seraphim thronged the air;
But His mother only, in her maiden bliss,
Worshipped the beloved with a kiss.

What can I give Him, poor as I am?
If I were a shepherd, I would bring a lamb;
If I were a Wise Man, I would do my part;
Yet what I can I give Him: give my heart.

The Oxen

Thomas Hardy

Christmas Eve, and twelve of the clock.
"Now they are all on their knees,"
An elder said as we sat in a flock
By the embers in hearthside ease.

We pictured the meek mild creatures where
They dwelt in their strawy pen,
Nor did it occur to one of us there
To doubt they were kneeling then.

So fair a fancy few would weave
In these years! Yet, I feel,
If someone said on Christmas Eve,
'Come; see the oxen kneel,

'In the lonely barton by yonder coomb
Our childhood used to know,'
I should go with him in the gloom,
Hoping it might be so.

The North Wind Doth Blow

Traditional

The north wind doth blow,
And we shall have snow,
And what will poor robin do then, poor thing?
He'll sit in a barn,
And keep himself warm,
And hide his head under his wing,
Poor thing.

Blow, Blow, Thou Winter Wind

From As You Like It *by William Shakespeare*

Blow, blow, thou winter wind,
Thou art not so unkind
As man's ingratitude;
Thy tooth is not so keen,
Because thou art not seen,
Although thy breath be rude.
Heigh-ho, sing heigh-ho! Unto the green holly,
Most friendship is feigning, most loving mere folly.
Then heigh-ho the holly!
This life is most jolly.

Blow, Blow, Thou Winter Wind

Freeze, freeze, thou bitter sky,
That dost not bite so nigh
As benefits forgot;
Though thou the waters warp,
Thy sting is not so sharp
As friend rememb'red not.
Heigh-ho, sing heigh-ho! Unto the green holly,
Most friendship is feigning, most loving mere folly.
Then heigh-ho the holly!
This life is most jolly.

Snow Flakes

Henry Wadsworth Longfellow

Out of the bosom of the air,
Out of the cloud-folds of her garments shaken,
Over the woodlands brown and bare,
Over the harvest-fields forsaken,
Silent, and soft, and slow
Descends the snow.

Even as our cloudy fancies take
Suddenly shape in some divine expression,
Even as the troubled heart doth make
In the white countenance confession,
The troubled sky reveals
The grief it feels.

This is the poem of the air,
Slowly in silent syllables recorded;
This is the secret of despair,
Long in its cloudy bosom hoarded,
Now whispered and revealed
To wood and field.

A Catch by the Hearth

Anonymous

Sing we all merrily
Christmas is here,
The day that we love best
Of the days in the year.

Bring forth the holly,
The box, and the bay,
Deck out our cottage
For glad Christmas-day.

Sing we all merrily
Draw around the fire,
Sister and brother,
Grandsire, and sire.

The Christmas Pudding

Anonymous

Into the basin
Put the plums,
Stir–about, stir–about,
Stir–about!

Next the good
White flour comes,
Stir–about, stir–about,
Stir–about!

Sugar and peel
And eggs and spice,
Stir–about, stir–about,
Stir–about!

Mix them and fix them
And cook them twice,
Stir–about, stir–about,
Stir–about!

Voices in the Mist

Alfred, Lord Tennyson

The time draws near the birth of Christ;
The moon is hid; the night is still;
The Christmas bells from hill to hill
Answer each other in the mist.

Four voices of four hamlets round,
From far and near, on mead and moor,
Swell out and fail, as if a door
Were shut between me and the sound;

Each voice four changes on the wind,
That now dilate and now decrease,
Peace and goodwill, goodwill and peace,
Peace and goodwill, to all mankind.

The Holy Night

Elizabeth Barrett Browning

We sate among the stalls at Bethlehem;
The dumb kine from their fodder turning them,
Softened their horn'd faces,
To almost human gazes
Toward the newly Born:
The simple shepherds from the star-lit brooks
Brought visionary looks,
As yet in their astonished hearing rung
The strange sweet angel-tongue:
The magi of the East in sandals worn,
Knelt reverent, sweeping round,
With long pale beards, their gifts upon the ground,
The incense, myrrh, and gold
These baby hands were impotent to hold:
So let all earthlies and celestials wait
Upon thy royal state.
Sleep, sleep my kingly One!

The Three Kings

An extract by Henry Wadsworth Longfellow

Three Kings came riding from far away,
Melchior and Gaspar and Baltasar;
Three Wise Men out of the East were they,
And they travelled by night and they slept by day,
For their guide was a beautiful, wonderful star.

The star was so beautiful, large and clear,
That all the other stars of the sky
Became a white mist in the atmosphere,
And by this they knew that the coming was near
Of the Prince foretold in the prophecy.

The Three Kings

Three caskets they bore on their saddle-bows,
Three caskets of gold with golden keys;
Their robes were of crimson silk with rows
Of bells and pomegranates and furbelows,
Their turbans like blossoming almond-trees.

So they rode away; and the star stood still,
The only one in the grey of morn;
Yes, it stopped – it stood still of its own free will,
Right over Bethlehem on the hill,
The city of David, where Christ was born.

And the Three Kings rode through the gate and the guard,
Through the silent street, till their horses turned
And neighed as they entered the great inn-yard;
But the windows were closed, and the doors were barred,
And only a light in the stable burned.

And cradled there in the scented hay,
In the air made sweet by the breath of kine,
The little child in the manger lay,
The child, that would be king one day
Of a kingdom not human, but divine.

The Burning Babe

Robert Southwell

As I in hoary winter's night stood shivering in the snow,
Surprised I was with sudden heat which made my heart to glow;
And lifting up a fearful eye to view what fire was near,
A pretty babe all burning bright did in the air appear;
Who, though scorched with excessive heat,
such floods of tears did shed,
As though his floods should quench his flames,
which with his tears were fed.

"Alas," quoth he, "but newly born, in fiery heats I fry,
Yet none approach to warm their hearts, or feel my fire but I!
My faultless breast the furnace is, the fuel wounding thorns,
Love is the fire, and sighs the smoke, the ashes shame and scorns;
The fuel justice layeth on, and mercy blows the coals,
The metal in this furnace wrought are men's defiled souls,
For which, as now on fire I am to work them to their good,
So will I melt into a bath to wash them in my blood."
With this he vanished out of sight and swiftly shrunk away,
And straight I called unto mind that it was Christmas Day.

Songs & Carols

Some people say that the first-ever Christmas song
was sung by angels the night that Jesus was born:
*And suddenly there was with the angel a multitude of the heavenly
host praising God and saying, "Glory to God in the highest,
and on Earth peace among men with whom he is pleased!"*
(Luke 2: 13-15)

Christmas songs grew popular in medieval times, when
groups of entertainers in Europe performed musical plays
based on Bible stories, such as the nativity. Many early carols
were pagan folk songs rewritten with Christian elements.

The custom of singing carols from house to house began in
the 15th century, when it was called wassailing. Several carols
that we still sing today, such as 'God Rest Ye, Merry
Gentlemen' and 'The First Noel' date from that time. Other
favourites were composed in the 18th and 19th centuries,
when the tradition of carolling was at its most popular.

Today, Christmas is not complete without a festive sing-song,
whether it is joining in a chorus of 'Silent Night' at church or
humming 'Jingle Bells' while doing your Christmas shopping.

Deck the Halls

Traditional

Deck the halls with boughs of holly,
Fa-la-la-la-la la-la-la-la.
'Tis the season to be jolly,
Fa-la-la-la-la la-la-la-la.
Don we now our gay apparel,
Fa-la-la-la-la la-la-la-la.
Troll the ancient Yuletide carol,
Fa-la-la-la-la la-la-la-la.

See the blazing Yule before us,
Fa-la-la-la-la la-la-la-la.
Strike the harp and join the chorus,
Fa-la-la-la-la la-la-la-la.
Follow me in merry measure,
Fa-la-la-la-la la-la-la-la.
While I tell of Yuletide treasure,
Fa-la-la-la-la la-la-la-la.

Fast away the old year passes,
Fa-la-la-la-la la-la-la-la.
Hail the new year, lads and lasses,
Fa-la-la-la-la la-la-la-la.
Sing we joyous all together,
Fa-la-la-la-la la-la-la-la.
Heedless of the wind and weather,
Fa-la-la-la-la la-la-la-la.

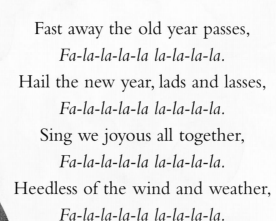

The Twelve Days of Christmas

Traditional

On the first day of Christmas my true love sent to me,
A partridge in a pear tree.

On the second day of Christmas
my true love sent to me,
Two turtle doves, and a partridge in a pear tree.

On the third day of Christmas my true love sent to me,
Three French hens, two turtle doves,
And a partridge in a pear tree.

On the fourth day of Christmas
my true love sent to me,
Four calling birds, three French hens,
Two turtle doves, and a partridge in a pear tree.

On the fifth day of Christmas my true love sent to me,
Five gold rings, four calling birds, three French hens,
Two turtle doves, and a partridge in a pear tree.

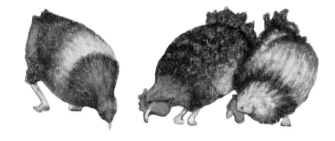

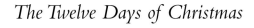

The Twelve Days of Christmas

On the sixth day of Christmas my true love sent to me,
Six geese a-laying, five gold rings, four calling birds,
Three French hens, two turtle doves, and a partridge in a pear tree.

On the seventh day of Christmas my true love sent to me,
Seven swans a-swimming, six geese a-laying, five gold rings,
Four calling birds, three French hens, two turtle doves,
And a partridge in a pear tree.

On the eighth day of Christmas my true love sent to me,
Eight maids a-milking, seven swans a-swimming, six geese a-laying,
Five gold rings, four calling birds, three French hens,
Two turtle doves, and a partridge in a pear tree.

On the ninth day of Christmas my true love sent to me,
Nine drummers drumming, eight maids a-milking,
seven swans a-swimming, six geese a-laying,
Five gold rings, four calling birds,
Three French hens, two turtle doves,
And a partridge in a pear tree.

The Twelve Days of Christmas

On the tenth day of Christmas my true love sent to me,
Ten pipers piping, nine drummers drumming,
Eight maids a-milking, seven swans a-swimming,
Six geese a-laying, five gold rings, Four calling birds,
Three French hens, two turtle doves,
And a partridge in a pear tree.

On the eleventh day of Christmas my true love sent to me,
Eleven ladies dancing, ten pipers piping,
Nine drummers drumming, eight maids a-milking,
Seven swans a-swimming, six geese a-laying, five gold rings,
Four calling birds, three French hens, two turtle doves,
And a partridge in a pear tree.

On the twelfth day of Christmas my true love sent to me,
Twelve lords a-leaping, eleven ladies dancing, ten pipers piping,
Nine drummers drumming, eight maids a-milking,
Seven swans a-swimming, six geese a-laying, five gold rings,
Four calling birds, three French hens, two turtle doves,
And a partridge in a pear tree.

Christmas is Coming

Traditional

Christmas is coming,
The geese are getting fat;
Please to put a penny
In the old man's hat;
If you haven't got a penny,
Ha'penny will do.
If you haven't got a ha'penny,
God bless you.

Jingle Bells

James Pierpont

Dashing through the snow
In a one-horse open sleigh,
O'er the fields we go
Laughing all the way;
Bells on bob-tail ring
Making spirits bright,
What fun it is to ride and sing
A sleighing song tonight!

O! Jingle bells, jingle bells, jingle all the way!
O what fun it is to ride,
In a one-horse open sleigh, hey!
Jingle bells, jingle bells, jingle all the way!
O what fun it is to ride,
In a one-horse open sleigh!

I Saw Three Ships

Traditional

I saw three ships come sailing by,
Come sailing by, come sailing by,
I saw three ships come sailing by,
On New Year's Day in the morning.

And what do you think was in them then,
Was in them then, was in them then?
And what do you think was in them then,
On New Year's Day in the morning?

Three pretty girls were in them then,
Were in them then, were in them then,
Three pretty girls were in them then,
On New Year's Day in the morning.

Ding Dong Merrily on High

George Ratcliffe Woodward

Ding dong merrily on high,
In heav'n the bells are ringing:
Ding dong! verily the sky
Is riv'n with angels singing.
Gloria, Hosanna in excelsis!

E'en so here, below, below,
Let steeple bells be swungen:
And "I-o, i-o, i-o!"
By priest and people sungen.
Gloria, Hosanna in excelsis!

Pray you, dutifully prime
Your matin chime, ye ringers;
May you beautifully rime
Your evetime song, ye singers.
Gloria, Hosanna in excelsis!

We Wish You a Merry Christmas

Traditional

We wish you a Merry Christmas,
We wish you a Merry Christmas,
We wish you a Merry Christmas,
And a Happy New Year!

Refrain
Good tidings we bring for you and your kin;
We wish you a Merry Christmas
And a Happy New Year!

Now bring us some figgy pudding,
Now bring us some figgy pudding,
Now bring us some figgy pudding,
And a cup of good cheer!

Refrain

We won't go until we get some
We won't go until we get some
We won't go until we get some
So bring it out here!

Refrain

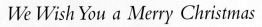

We Wish You a Merry Christmas

We all know that Santa's coming,
We all know that Santa's coming,
We all know that Santa's coming,
    And soon will be here.

Refrain

We wish you a Merry Christmas;
We wish you a Merry Christmas;
We wish you a Merry Christmas
    And a Happy New Year.

Refrain

Away in a Manger

Anonymous

Away in a manger, no crib for a bed,
The little Lord Jesus laid down his sweet head.
The stars in the sky looked down where He lay,
The little Lord Jesus, asleep on the hay.

The cattle are lowing, the poor Baby wakes,
But little Lord Jesus, no crying He makes,
I love Thee, Lord Jesus, look down from the sky,
And stay by my cradle till morning is nigh.

Be near me, Lord Jesus, I ask Thee to stay
Close by me forever, and love me, I pray,
Bless all the dear children in Thy tender care,
And take us to heaven, to live with Thee there.

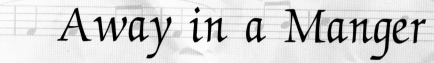

O Come All Ye Faithful

John Francis Wade

O Come All Ye Faithful,	Sing, choirs of angels,
Joyful and triumphant,	Sing in exultation,
O come ye, o come ye	Sing all ye citizens
To Bethlehem;	Of heaven above;
Come and behold Him,	Glory to god
Born the King of angels;	In the highest;
O come let us adore Him,	O come let us adore Him,
O come let us adore Him,	O come let us adore Him,
O come let us adore Him,	O come let us adore Him,
Christ the Lord.	Christ the Lord.

Silent Night

Joseph Mohr

Silent night! Holy night!
All is calm, all is bright.
'Round yon virgin, mother and child.
Holy infant, so tender and mild,
Sleep in heavenly peace,
Sleep in heavenly peace.

Silent night! Holy night!
Shepherds quake at the sight!
Glories stream from heaven afar,
Heav'nly hosts sing Alleluia!
Christ the Saviour is born!
Christ the Saviour is born!

Silent night! Holy night!
Son of God love's pure light.
Radiant beams from Thy holy face
With dawn of redeeming grace,
Jesus, Lord at Thy birth,
Jesus, Lord at Thy birth.

We Three Kings of Orient Are

John H Hopkins

We three kings of Orient are;
Bearing gifts we traverse afar,
Field and fountain, moor and mountain,
Following yonder star.

Refrain

O, star of wonder, star of light,
Star with royal beauty bright,
Westward leading, still proceeding,
Guide us to thy perfect light.

Born a King on Bethlehem's plain,
Gold I bring to crown Him again,
King forever, ceasing never,
Over us all to reign.

Refrain

Frankincense to offer have I;
Incense owns a Deity nigh;
Prayer and praising, voices raising,
Worshipping God on high.

Refrain

Myrrh is mine, its bitter perfume
Breathes a life of gathering gloom;
Sorrowing, sighing, bleeding, dying,
Sealed in the stone cold tomb.

Refrain

Glorious now behold Him arise;
King and God and sacrifice;
Alleluia, Alleluia,
Sounds through the earth and skies.

Refrain

The Holly and the Ivy

Anonymous

The holly and the ivy,
When they are both full grown,
Of all the trees that are in the wood,
The holly bears the crown.

Chorus
The rising of the sun,
And the running of the deer,
The playing of the merry organ,
Sweet singing in the choir.

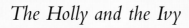

The Holly and the Ivy

The holly bears a blossom,
As white as the lily flower,
And Mary bore sweet Jesus Christ
To be our sweet Saviour.

Chorus

The holly bears a berry,
As red as any blood,
And Mary bore sweet Jesus Christ
To do poor sinners good.

Chorus

The holly bears a prickle,
As sharp as any thorn,
And Mary bore sweet Jesus Christ
On Christmas Day in the morn.

Chorus

The holly bears a bark,
As bitter as any gall,
And Mary bore sweet Jesus Christ
For to redeem us all.

Chorus

Index of first lines and titles

First lines appear in italic